Parachu

To make a toy parachute, you will need:

a plastic bag

rulers

scissors

string

a clothes-peg or
some other weight

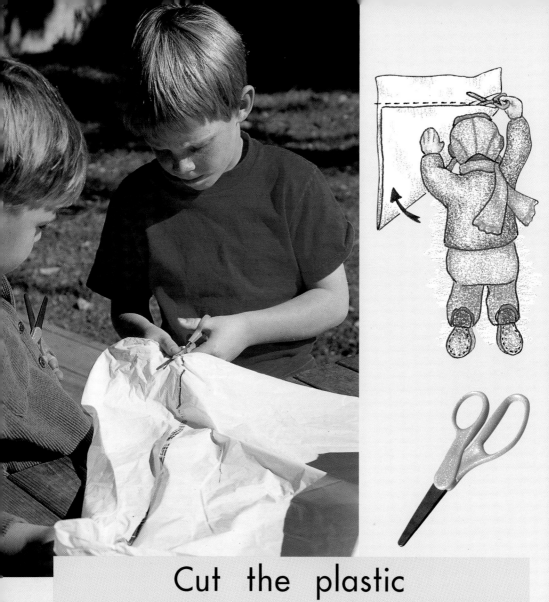

Cut the plastic
into a square.

Cut a small hole
in each corner.

Don't make the holes
too close to the edge.

Cut the string into
four even lengths.

Tie a string to each corner of the plastic.

Bring the ends
of all four strings
together evenly.

Tie a knot in the end
of the strings.

Add a weight to
the parachute.

You can use a clothes-peg,
a pine cone,
a reel,
or a small toy.

Fold your parachute into four parts.

Toss it up in the air
and watch it
come down.

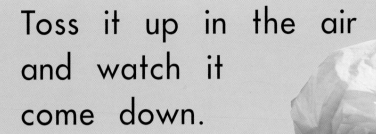

What does the wind do to your parachute?

Can you make
your parachute land
on a bull's-eye?

Use your parachute
for a game of catch.

Send a message to a friend.